Crocheted Bears

Val Pierce

Search Press

First published in Great Britain 2011
Search Press Limited
Wellwood, North Farm Road,
Tunbridge Wells, Kent TN2 3DR

Reprinted 2012

Text copyright © Val Pierce 2011

Photographs by Debbie Patterson at
Search Press Studios

Photographs and design copyright
© Search Press Ltd 2011

ISBN: 978-1-84448-633-5

Suppliers

If you have difficulty in obtaining any of the
materials and equipment mentioned in this book,
then please visit the Search Press website for
details of suppliers: www.searchpress.com

Printed in Malaysia

Dedication
All the little bears in this book have
been such fun to create and I would
like to dedicate this book to the
wonderful staff of Search Press, from
whom came much of my inspiration!

Contents

Introduction 4

The basic bear 6

Mary Party Bear 8

Sweet Angel Bear 10

Betsy Birthday Bear 12

Katie Wedding Bear 14

Andrew Bridegroom Bear 16

Jeffrey the Dancing Bear 18

Edward Book Bear 20

Sparkles the Fairy Bear 22

Mazzy the Keep-fit Bear 24

Belinda Butterfly Bear 26

Anthony Garden Bear 28

Caroline in the Kitchen 30

Roz the Artist Bear 32

Musical Briony Bear 34

Bernie the Christmas Elf 36

Paul the Panda Bear 38

Juan the Flamenco Bear 40

Sophie the Swimmer 42

Ali the Baby Bear 44

Susie the Sunshine Bear 46

Introduction

Teddy bears have been around for over a hundred years and appeal to people of all ages. With this in mind, I have designed 20 tiny crocheted bears, each made from the same basic pattern and dressed in a different outfit. There's a keep-fit enthusiast, a gardener, a cook and an artist, to name just a few, and all the clothes and accessories can be easily adapted to make characters of your own.

Each little bear is approximately 10cm (4in) high and sits nicely in the palm of your hand. Though suitable for people of all ages, they are not, strictly speaking, playthings and are therefore not suitable for very young children and babies. They do, however, make unique and enduring gifts that your friends and family will treasure for many years to come.

The patterns are a little intricate in places but relatively simple to follow and, I am sure you will agree, the finished result will be well worth the effort.

Happy crocheting!

The basic bear

These are the instructions for making the basic crocheted bear. When working the pieces, it is a good idea to mark the beginning of each round to avoid losing or even gaining stitches.

Stuff each part with small amounts of filling as you work; avoid over-stuffing.

American and British crochet terminology
In all the patterns, US terms are given first, followed by the UK terms afterwards in brackets. So US single crochet would be written as sc (UK dc) and US double crochet as dc (UK tr).

The most frequently used terms are:

American	British
slip stitch (sl st)	slip stitch (sl st)
chain stitch (ch)	chain stitch (ch)
single crochet (sc)	double crochet (dc)
half double crochet (hdc)	half treble crochet (htr)
double crochet (dc)	treble crochet (tr)
skip	miss
chain space (ch sp)	chain space (ch sp)
together (tog)	together (tog)

Materials
All the bears, their clothes and accessories are made using a size 2.50mm (US B-1, UK 13) crochet hook and a crisp no. 5 crochet cotton or, if you prefer, a fine 4-ply yarn. Two outfits – Ali the Baby Bear's clothes and Roz the Artist Bear's beret – use a no. 3 crochet cotton. Each bear will take approximately half a ball of crochet cotton in the main colour. For most of the clothes, features and accessories, oddments of yarn can be used. You will also need a small amount of fibrefill toy stuffing, and a darning needle for sewing up the bears and for the occasional piece of embroidery.

Measurements
Each bear measures approximately 11cm (4¼in) in height when sitting.

Tension/gauge
5 sc (UK dc) measure 2.5cm (1in) in width using the stated hook, though tension is not critical when making these bears if you are prepared to accept a small variation in size.

Instructions:

Head
Row 1: with the appropriate colour yarn, make 2 ch, 6 sc (UK dc) in 2nd ch from hook, join in a circle with a sl st.
Row 2: 1 ch, 2 sc (UK dc) in each sc (UK dc) all round, join with a sl st [12 sts].
Rows 3–5: work in sc (UK dc).
Join the contrasting yarn, if stated in the instructions, and proceed as follows:
Row 6: *1 sc (UK dc) in next sc (UK dc), 2 sc (UK dc) in next sc (UK dc)*, rep from * to * all round.
Rows 7 and 8: work in sc (UK dc).
Row 9: inc 6 sc (UK dc) evenly in row.
Rows 10–15: work in sc (UK dc).
Row 16: dec 6 sc (UK dc) evenly in row.
Row 17: work in sc (UK dc).
Row 18: dec 6 sc (UK dc) evenly in row.
Row 19: work in sc (UK dc).
Row 20: dec 4 sc (UK dc) evenly in row.
Break yarn and run through last row. Draw up and fasten off.

Body

Row 1: with the appropriate colour yarn, make 2 ch, work 6 sc (*UK dc*) in 2nd ch from hook, join with a sl st to form a tight circle.

Subsequent rows are all joined with a sl st unless otherwise stated.

Row 2: 2 sc (*UK dc*) in each dc (*UK dc*) all round, join as before [12 sts].

Row 3: *1 sc (*UK dc*) in next st, 2 sc (*UK dc*) in next sc (*UK dc*)*, rep from * to * all round [18 sts].

Row 4: *1 sc (*UK dc*) in each of next 2 sc (*UK dc*), 2 sc (*UK dc*) in next sc (*UK dc*)*, rep from * to * all round [24 sts].

Row 5: *1 sc (*UK dc*) in each of next 3 sc (*UK dc*), 2 sc (*UK dc*) in next sc (*UK dc*)*, rep from * to * all round [30 sts].

Rows 6–18: sc (*UK dc*).

Row 19: dec 6 sts evenly all round [24 sts].

Row 20: sc (*UK dc*).

Rep rows 19 and 20 until 6 sc (*UK dc*) rem. Finish stuffing the body, break yarn and run the thread through the last row. Draw up and fasten off.

Arms (make 2)

Row 1: with the appropriate colour yarn, make 2 ch, 7 sc (*UK dc*) in 2nd ch from hook, join in a tight circle with a sl st.

Row 2: 2 sc (*UK dc*) in each st, 14 sc (*UK dc*), join with a sl st.

Rows 3–14: sc (*UK dc*).

Row 15: *sc (*UK dc*) 2 tog, 1 sc (*UK dc*) in next sc (*UK dc*)*, rep from * to * all round.

Row 16: sc (*UK dc*) all round. Break yarn.
Complete the stuffing, pushing a little extra into the base of the arm to form the paw. Pull up to close. This is the top of the arm.

Legs (make 2)

The foot is shaped, so push a little extra stuffing into that area as you work.

Row 1: with the appropriate colour yarn, make 2 ch, 7 sc (*UK dc*) in 2nd ch from hook, join in a tight circle with a sl st.

Row 2: 2 sc (*UK dc*) in each st, 14 sc (*UK dc*), join with a sl st.

Row 3: *1 sc (*UK dc*), 2 sc (*UK dc*) in next st*, rep from * to *, working 1 sc (*UK dc*) in last st [20 sts].

Rows 4–6: sc (*UK dc*) all round.

Row 7: 7 sc (*UK dc*), [sc (*UK dc*) 2 tog] 3 times, 7 sc (*UK dc*).

Rows 8–17: sc (*UK dc*) all round.

Row 18: dec 3 sts evenly all round.

Row 19: sc (*UK dc*) all round.

Row 20: dec 3 sts evenly all round.

Break yarn, draw yarn through last row of sc (*UK dc*), draw up and fasten off.

Ears (make 2)

Row 1: with the appropriate colour yarn, make 2 ch, 7 sc (*UK dc*) in 2nd ch from hook, join into a circle.

Row 2: 2 sc (*UK dc*) in each sc (*UK dc*) all round.

Row 3: sc (*UK dc*) all round. Fasten off.

To make up

Work in all the loose ends. Sew the head firmly to the body. You can position the head at different angles to give the bear more character. Pin the ears on each side of the head, and when you are happy with their position, sew them on firmly. Embroider the nose and eyes on to the head of the bear, then stitch a straight line from the centre of the nose to the chin, and a thin line above the eyes to make the eyebrows. Sew the arms in position on either side of the bear's shoulders. Attach the legs, one on each side, in a sitting position. Make sure they are level so that your bear sits down properly.

Mary Party Bear

Materials and equipment:

Crochet hook size 2.50mm (US B-1, UK 13)

No. 5 crochet cotton – 1 ball of ecru, 1 ball of red

Small amount of crochet cotton in very light beige

Brown floss for embroidering features

Short strip of red sequins

Small piece of marabou in bright red

String of approx. 50 small pearl beads

Toy stuffing

Sewing needle and threads in colours to match crochet cotton

Instructions:

Make the bear following the basic instructions at the beginning of the book, using ecru for the head, body, arms and legs and very light beige for the muzzle and ears.

Dress back

Row 1: Using red crochet cotton, make 21 ch, 1 sc (UK dc) in 2nd ch from hook, 1 sc (UK dc) in each ch to end, turn [20 sts].
Row 2: 1 ch, 1 sc (UK dc) in each sc (UK dc) to end, turn.
Row 3: rep row 2.
Row 4: sc (UK dc) 2 tog at each end of row [18 sts].
Row 5: sc (UK dc) to end.
Rows 6 and 7: rep rows 4 and 5 [16 sts].
Rows 8–10: sc (UK dc) to end.
Row 11: sl st across 3 sc (UK dc), work until 3 sc (UK dc) rem, turn.*
Work on these 10 sts for a further 8 rows. Fasten off.
Make frill along bottom edge of dress by working 2 dc (UK tr) in each st all along the starting chain. Fasten off.

Dress front

Work as dress back to *.
Continue on these sts for a further 4 rows.
Next row: work across 2 sc (UK dc), turn.
Continue on these 2 sts until strap matches back to shoulder. Fasten off.
Miss centre 6 sc (UK dc), join in yarn and complete to match other strap.
Work frill along bottom edge as for dress back.

To make up

Work the bear's features in brown floss. Sew the side seams of the dress. Take the sequin strip and measure enough to go all round the bottom of the dress. Stitch it in place along the last row of sc (UK dc), sewing through the centre of each sequin. Slip the dress on to the bear and sew the shoulder seams. Place the string of pearls around the bear's neck and tie it off firmly at the centre back of the neck. To make the head dress, wrap a piece of sequin strip around the bear's head, overlap it slightly at the back and stitch the two ends together. Take a tiny piece of marabou and stitch it to the join. Position the head dress on the bear's head and sew it in place with a few stitches. Cut a short length of the marabou to make a feather boa and drape it around the bear's neck.

Sweet Angel Bear

Materials and equipment:

Crochet hook size 2.50mm (US B-1, UK 13)

No. 5 crochet cotton – 1 ball of pale blue

Small amounts of crochet cotton in mid blue, black, pale turquoise and white

Small amount of silver metallic yarn

Black floss for embroidering features

Short length of silver jewellery wire

Toy stuffing

Sewing needle and threads in colours to match crochet cotton

Instructions:

Make the bear following the basic instructions at the beginning of the book, using pale blue for the head, body, arms and legs and mid blue for the muzzle and ears.

Wings (make 4)

Row 1: Using white crochet cotton, make 3 ch. 9 dc (UK tr) in 3rd ch from hook, turn.
Row 2: 3 ch, 1 dc (UK tr) in first dc (UK tr), 2 dc (UK tr) in each of rem dc (UK tr), turn.
Row 3: 1 sc (UK dc) in each dc (UK tr) to end. Break white and join in metallic yarn. Work a further row of sc (UK dc) round the edge of the wing. Fasten off.

Skirt

Row 1: using pale turquoise, make 30 ch. Join with a sl st to beg of row, making sure you do not twist the chain.
Row 2: 1 ch, 1 sc (UK dc) in each ch to end, joining as before.
Row 3: 4 ch, miss 2 sc (UK dc), 1 sc (UK dc) in next sc (UK dc), *2 ch, miss 2 ch, 1 sc (UK dc) in next sc (UK dc)*. Rep from * to * all round, 2 ch, sl st to 2nd of 4 turning ch of previous row. Change to white yarn.
Row 4: sl st in first ch sp, 3 ch, [1 dc (UK tr), 2 ch, 2 dc (UK tr)] in same sp, *[2 dc (UK tr), 2 ch, 2 dc (UK tr)] in next sp*, rep from * to * all round, join in top of 3 ch at beg of row.
Row 5: rep row 4.
Row 6: change to pale turquoise and work row 5 again. Fasten off.
Join in metallic yarn and work edging as follows:
Row 7: *1 sc (UK dc) in each of next 2 dc (UK tr), picot in next sp, (3 ch, sl st in first of the 3 ch)*, rep from * to * all round, join with a sl st.

Halo

Row 1: Make 10 ch, join in a ring with a sl st, *5 ch, 1 sc (UK dc)*, rep from * to * 8 times, join with a sl st to beg of row.
Row 2: *5 sc (UK dc) in 5 ch loop, sl st in next sc (UK dc)*, rep from * to * all round, join with a sl st to beg of row. Fasten off.

To make up

Work in the ends on all the pieces. Sew the wings together in pairs. Join them in the centre and place them on the bear's back level with the tops of the arms. Sew them firmly in place. Slip the skirt on to the bear with the join at centre back. Secure with a few stitches. Take a length of silver jewellery wire and thread it around the inner edge of the halo. Twist the ends of the wire together and push them firmly in the bear's head towards the back. Arrange the halo in a pleasing shape.

Betsy Birthday Bear

Materials and equipment:

Crochet hook size 2.50mm (US B-1, UK 13)

No. 5 crochet cotton – 1 ball of light beige, 1 ball of deep pink

Small amounts of crochet cotton in mid brown

Black floss for embroidering features

4 tiny ribbon roses

Approx. 30 tiny crystal beads

Small piece of pink net for hat

Toy stuffing

Sewing needle and threads in colours to match crochet cotton

Instructions:

Make the bear following the basic instructions at the beginning of the book, using light beige for the head, body, arms and legs and mid brown for the muzzle and ears.

Dress skirt

Row 1: using deep pink yarn, make 30 ch, join with a sl st to beg of row, making sure you do not twist the chain.
Row 2: 1 ch, 1 sc (*UK dc*) in each ch to end, joining as before.

Row 3: *3 ch, miss 1 sc (*UK dc*), 1 sc (*UK dc*) in next sc (*UK dc*)*, rep from * to * all round, join in 3 ch sp at beg of row.
Row 4: *3 ch, 1 sc (*UK dc*) in next 3 ch loop*, rep from * to * all round, joining as before.
Row 5: work as row 4.
Row 6: 3 ch, 4 dc (*UK tr*) in same loop as join, 5 dc (*UK tr*) in each following 3 ch loop, join with a sl st to top of 3 ch at beg of row. Fasten off. Fold skirt in half with join at centre back.

Dress bodice

Row 1: working along starting ch, miss first 10 ch, join yarn into next ch, 1 sc (*UK dc*) in each of next 10 ch, turn.
Row 2: 1 ch, 1 sc (*UK dc*) in each sc (*UK dc*) to end, working last sc (*UK dc*) in place where yarn was joined in, turn.
Rows 3 and 4: sc (*UK dc*). Fasten off.

Crocheted flower for hat

Row 1: using deep pink yarn, make 4 ch, join in a circle with a sl st.
Row 2: *4 ch, 1 sc (*UK dc*) in circle*, rep from * to * 5 times, join with a sl st to beg of row. Fasten off.

To make up

Work in the ends on all the pieces. Make a chain long enough to reach from each corner of the bodice and around the bear's neck. Sew the chain to one corner of the bodice. Slip the dress on to the bear and secure the chain on the other side of the bodice. Sew a deep pink ribbon rose to the centre front of the dress. Thread the crystal beads on to a double length of strong thread to make the necklace. Tie the cotton firmly at the back of the bear's neck and secure. To make the hat, cut a small circle of pink net slightly bigger than the crocheted flower. Gather the circle slightly in the centre. Place the flower on top of the net, take three ribbon roses and place these in the centre of the flower. Now stitch through the roses, flower and net to hold them all together. Sew the hat to the top of the bear's head.

13

Katie Wedding Bear

Materials and equipment:

Crochet hook size 2.50mm (US B-1, UK 13)

No. 5 crochet cotton – 1 ball of cream

Small amounts of crochet cotton in mid brown

Black floss for embroidering features

Toy stuffing

Piece of cream net for veil, 5 x 8cm
(2 x 3¼in)

7 small yellow and mauve paper roses

12 small white beads for collar

Sewing needle and threads in colours to
match crochet cotton

Instructions:

Make the bear following the basic instructions
at the beginning of the book, using cream for
the head, body, arms and legs and mid brown
for the muzzle and ears.

Skirt

Row 1: using cream, make 30 ch, join with a sl
st to beg of row, making sure you do not twist
the chain.
Row 2: (RS) 1 ch, 1 sc (UK dc) in each ch to end,
joining as before.
Row 3: 4 ch, miss 2 sc (UK dc), 1 sc (UK dc) in
next sc (UK dc), *2 ch, miss 2 ch, 1 sc (UK dc)
in next sc (UK dc)*, rep from * to * all round
ending last rep, 2 ch, miss 2 ch, sl st in 2nd of 4
ch at beg of row.
Row 4: sl st in first ch sp, 3 ch, [1 dc (UK tr), 2 ch,
2 dc (UK tr)] in same sp, *[2 dc (UK tr), 2 ch, 2 dc
(UK tr)] in next sp*, rep from * to * all round, join
in top of 3 ch at beg of row.
Rows 5 and 6: rep row 4.
Turn, then work edging from WS:
1 dc (UK tr) in next st, sl st in next st, rep from
* to * all round, working in all sts and sps, join
with a sl st to beg of row. Fasten off.

Crocheted flower for bouquet

Row 1: using cream yarn, make 8 ch and join in
ring with a sl st.
Row 2: *4 ch, 1 sc (UK dc) in ring*, rep from * to
* 5 times, join with a sl st.
Row 3: *[1 sc (UK dc), 1 dc (UK tr), 1 sc (UK dc)]
in next 4 ch loop, sl st in next sc (UK dc)*, rep
from * to * all round and join with a sl st to beg
of row. Fasten off.

Crocheted flower for head dress

Row 1: using cream yarn, make 4 ch and join in
a circle with a sl st.
Row 2: *4 ch, 1 sc (UK dc) in circle*, rep from
* to * 5 times, join with a sl st to beg of row.
Fasten off.

Collar

Row 1: using cream yarn, make 24 ch, 1 sc (UK
dc) in 2nd ch from hook, 1 sc (UK dc) in each ch
to end, turn.
Row 2: 1 ch, *sl st in next sc (UK dc), 1 dc (UK tr)
in next sc (UK dc)*, rep from * to * along row.
Fasten off.

To make up

For the head dress, use a needle and matching thread to gather the net across one short edge. Push two paper roses through the centre of the crocheted flower and twist the wire backs of the flowers together to secure them. Attach the gathered net to the crocheted head dress and arrange it on the bear's head. Secure with a few stitches. Take the collar and sew a tiny white bead to each point on the last row. Place the collar around the bear's neck and secure it at the centre back. For the bouquet, take five paper roses and arrange them in a neat bunch. Twist the wire backs together and thread them through the centre of the crocheted flower. Using a needle and matching thread, stitch the flowers to the crochet. Slip the skirt on to the bear with the join at the centre back and secure with a few stitches. Sew the bear's paws to the bouquet on each side.

Andrew Bridegroom Bear

Materials and equipment:

Crochet hook size 2.50mm (US B-1, UK 13)

No. 5 crochet cotton – 1 ball of beige

Small amounts of crochet cotton in black, brown and cream

Small amount of pale grey 4-ply yarn

Black floss for embroidering features

Small pearl bead for tie pin

1 yellow paper rose

Narrow satin ribbon in pale grey

Toy stuffing

Sewing needle and threads in colours to match crochet cotton

Instructions:

Make the bear following the basic instructions at the beginning of the book, using beige for the head, body, arms and legs and brown for the muzzle and ears.

Top hat crown

Row 1: using grey, make 2 ch, 6 sc (*UK dc*) in 2nd ch, join with a sl st.
Row 2: 2 sc (*UK dc*) in each sc (*UK dc*). Join with a sl st to beg of row.

Row 3: *1 sc (*UK dc*) in next sc (*UK dc*), 2 sc (*UK dc*) in next sc (*UK dc*)*, rep from * to * all round. Join as before. Fasten off.

Top hat side

Row 1: using grey, make 6 ch, 1 sc (*UK dc*) in 2nd ch from hook, 1 sc (*UK dc*) in each ch to end, turn.
Row 2: 1 sc (*UK dc*) into each sc (*UK dc*) to end, turn.
Continue on these 5 sts for a further 22 rows. Fasten off.

Hat brim

Row 1: using grey, make 27 ch, join in a circle with a sl st, making sure you do not twist the chain.
Row 2: 1 sc (*UK dc*) in each ch all round, join with a sl st to beg of row.
Row 3: 1 sc (1dc) in first sc (*UK dc*), *2 sc (*UK dc*) in next sc (*UK dc*), 1 sc (*UK dc*) in next sc (*UK dc*)*, rep from * to * all round, join as before.
Row 4: sl st in each sc (*UK dc*) all round. Fasten off.

Waistcoat

Row 1: using black, make 30 ch, 1 sc (*UK dc*) in 2nd ch from hook, 1 sc (*UK dc*) in each ch to end.
Rows 2–4: work 3 rows sc (*UK dc*).
Row 5: work across 6 sc (*UK dc*), turn.
Row 6: work to last 2 sc (*UK dc*), sc (*UK dc*) 2 tog.
Row 7: sc (*UK dc*) 2 tog, work to end.
Row 8: work to last 2 sc (*UK dc*), sc (*UK dc*) 2 tog.
Row 9: sc (*UK dc*) 2 tog, work to end [2 sts].
Rows 10 and 11: work 2 rows sc (*UK dc*). Fasten off.
Rejoin yarn, miss 4 sc (*UK dc*), join to next sc (*UK dc*), work 10 sc (*UK dc*), turn and continue on these sts for back.
Work 8 rows sc (*UK dc*). Fasten off.
Next row: miss 4 sc (*UK dc*), rejoin yarn to rem sts and work other front to match, reversing shaping.

Cravat

Row 1: using cream, make 7 ch, 1 sc (*UK dc*) in 2nd ch from hook, 1 sc (*UK dc*) in each ch to end, turn.
Row 2: 1 ch, 1 sc (*UK dc*) in each sc (*UK dc*) to end, turn.
Rep row 2 until piece is 12cm (4¾in) long. Fasten off.

To make up

Work in the ends on all the pieces. Take the side piece of the top hat and join the two short ends together to form a cylinder. Place the crown on to one end of the cylinder and stitch it carefully in place. Slip the brim over the hat, position it carefully and then stitch it in place. Take the ribbon and cut a piece to fit around the hat, leaving a tiny overlap. Stitch it in place. Catch the top hat to the bear's paw with a few stitches. Tie the cravat around the bear's neck, pouch slightly and sew a pearl bead to the centre to represent a tie pin. Sew the shoulder seams on the waistcoat and slip it on to the bear. Arrange the cravat under the waistcoat. Catch the waistcoat together at the front edge with a few stitches and attach a paper rose. Personalise your bear by attaching a suitable button or charm to one of his paws.

Jeffrey the Dancing Bear

Materials and equipment:

Crochet hook size 2.50mm (US B-1, UK 13)

No. 5 crochet cotton – 1 ball of mid blue

Small amounts of crochet cotton in light blue, black and white

Black floss for embroidering features

Small amount of metallic yarn in silver

Cocktail stick

Small piece of narrow black satin ribbon for hat band

Toy stuffing

Craft glue

Sewing needle and threads in colours to match crochet cotton

Instructions:

Make the bear following the basic instructions at the beginning of the book, using mid blue for the head, body, arms and legs and light blue for the muzzle and ears.

Top hat crown

Row 1: using black yarn, make 2 ch, work 6 sc (UK dc) in 2nd ch, join with a sl st.
Row 2: 2 sc (UK dc) in each sc (UK dc). Join with a sl st to beg of row.
Row 3: *1 sc (UK dc) in next sc (UK dc), 2 sc (UK dc) in next sc (UK dc)*, rep from * to * all round and join as before. Fasten off.

Top hat side

Row 1: using black yarn, make 6 ch, 1 sc (UK dc) in 2nd ch from hook, 1 sc (UK dc) in each ch to end, turn.
Row 2: 1 sc (UK dc) in each sc (UK dc) to end, turn.
Continue on these 5 sts for a further 22 rows. Fasten off.

Brim of hat

Row 1: using black yarn, make 27 ch, join in a circle with a sl st, making sure you do not twist the chain.
Row 2: 1 sc (UK dc) in each ch, join with a sl st to beg of row.

Row 3: 1 sc (UK dc) in first sc (UK dc), *2 sc (UK dc) in next sc (UK dc), 1 sc (UK dc) in next sc (UK dc)*, rep from * to * all round, join as before.
Row 4: sl st in each sc (UK dc) all round. Fasten off.

Bow tie

Using white, make 26 ch, 1 sc (UK dc) in 2nd ch from hook, 1 sc (UK dc) in each ch to end. Fasten off.

Bow

Using white, make 5 ch, 1 sc (UK dc) in 2nd ch from hook, 1 sc (UK dc) in each ch to end.
Next row: 1 ch, 1 sc (UK dc) in each sc (UK dc) to end.
Rep last row 12 times. Fasten off.

Cane

With brown, make 20 ch, turn, 1 sc (UK dc) in 2nd ch from hook, 1 sc (UK dc) in each ch to end. Fasten off.

To make up

Work in the ends on all the pieces. Take the side piece of the top hat and join the two short ends together to form a cylinder. Place the crown on to one end of the cylinder and stitch it carefully in place. Slip the brim over the hat, position it carefully then stitch it in place. Take the ribbon and cut a piece to fit around the hat, leaving a tiny overlap. Stitch it in place. Stuff the hat lightly and sew it in place on the

bear's head. Take the bow and sew the two short ends together. Fold it in half with the join at the centre back. Run a thread through from top to bottom at the centre point and draw it up to form a bow shape. Sew the bow to the centre of the bow tie. Place it around the bear's neck and secure. Place the cocktail stick on to the piece of brown crochet and oversew the two sides together to enclose the wood. Snip off the two sharp points. Wind some metallic thread around one end of the stick to form the silver top. Glue it in place.

Edward Book Bear

Materials and equipment:

Crochet hook size 2.50mm (US B-1, UK 13)

No. 5 crochet cotton – 1 ball of mid brown

Small amounts of crochet cotton in dark brown, light blue, mid blue, cream, yellow and green

Black floss for embroidering features

Toy stuffing

Sewing needle and threads in colours to match crochet cotton

Instructions:

Make the bear following the basic instructions at the beginning of the book, using mid brown for the head, body, arms and legs and dark brown for the muzzle and ears.

Waistcoat

Row 1: using mid blue, make 30 ch, 1 sc (*UK dc*) in 2nd ch from hook, 1 sc (*UK dc*) in each ch to end.

Rows 2–4: work 3 rows sc (*UK dc*).

Row 5: work across 6 sc (*UK dc*), turn.

Row 6: work to last 2 sc (*UK dc*), sc (*UK dc*) 2 tog.

Row 7: sc (*UK dc*) 2 tog, work to end.

Row 8: work to last 2 sc (*UK dc*), sc (*UK dc*) 2 tog.

Row 9: sc (*UK dc*) 2 tog, work to end [2 sts].

Rows 10 and 11: work 2 rows sc (*UK dc*). Fasten off.

Rejoin yarn, miss 4 sc (*UK dc*), join to next sc (*UK dc*), work 10 sc (*UK dc*), turn and continue on these sts for the back.

Work 8 rows sc (*UK dc*). Fasten off.

Miss 4 sc (*UK dc*), rejoin yarn to rem sts and work other front to match, reversing shaping.

Book covers (make 3, or any number you wish)

Row 1: using any colour you wish, make 8 ch, 1 sc (*UK dc*) in 2nd ch from hook, 1 sc (*UK dc*) in each ch to end, turn.

Row 2: 1 ch, 1 sc (*UK dc*) in each sc (*UK dc*) to end, turn.

Rep row 2 12 times. Fasten off.

Book pages (make 2 for large book; 1 for smaller books)

Row 1: using cream, make 7 ch, 1 sc (*UK dc*) in 2nd ch from hook, 1 sc (*UK dc*) in each ch to end, turn.

Row 2: 1 ch, 1 sc (*UK dc*) in each sc (*UK dc*) to end, turn.

Rep row 2 10 times. Fasten off.

To make up

Work in the ends on all the pieces. Join the shoulder seams on the waistcoat and slip it on to the bear. For the large, open book, place one set of pages on to a cover, and stitch it in place all round and down the centre. Attach another set of pages by sewing down the centre, then slightly fold the pages and catch them down on each side. For the closed books, fold a set of pages in half and lightly stuff before sewing them up. Place the pages inside a cover and fold the cover over, again catching in place around the outside edges. Using black floss or brown crochet cotton, embroider details on the spines and covers of the books.

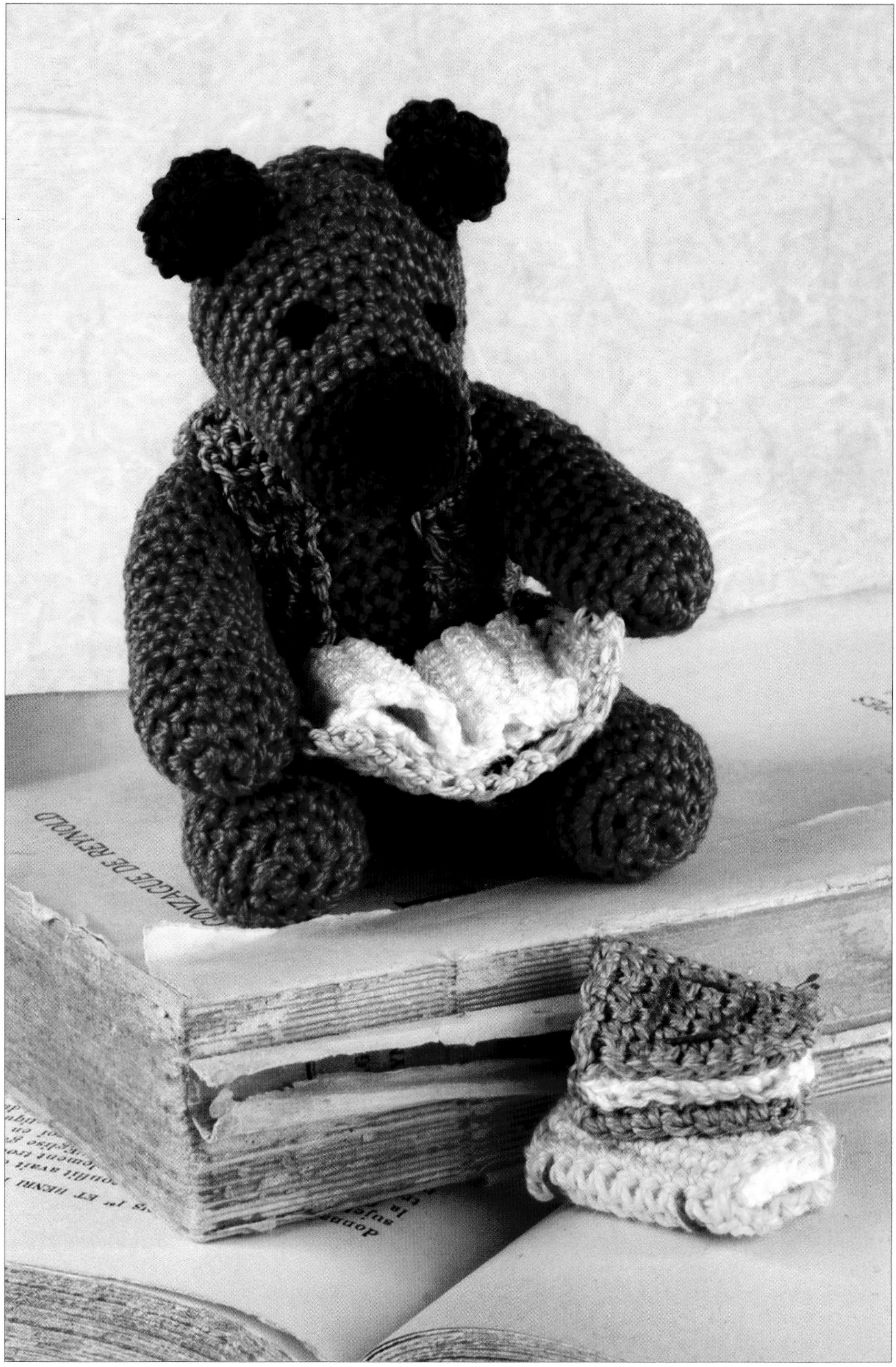

Sparkles the Fairy Bear

Materials and equipment:

Crochet hook size 2.50mm (US B-1, UK 13)

No. 5 crochet cotton – 1 ball of mid pink

Small amount of crochet cotton in dark pink

Small amount of gold metallic yarn

Dark brown floss for embroidering features

Toy stuffing

7 small sequin stars

Piece of pink net for skirt, 18 x 12cm (7 x 4¾in)

Cocktail stick

3 adhesive gold, sparkly stars

Sewing needle and threads in colours to match
crochet cotton

Craft glue

Instructions:

Make the bear following the basic instructions
at the beginning of the book, using mid pink
for the head, body, arms and legs and dark pink
for the muzzle and ears.

Wings (make 2)

Row 1: using gold metallic yarn, make 3 ch, 9 dc
(UK tr) in 3rd ch from hook, turn.
Row 2: 3 ch, 1 dc (UK tr) in first dc (UK tr), 2 dc
(UK tr) in each rem dc (UK tr), turn.
Row 3: 1 sc (UK dc) in each dc (UK tr) to end.
Fasten off.

Skirt

Take the piece of net and fold it in half
lengthwise, the folded edge forming the
bottom of the skirt. Using a sewing needle
and matching thread, lightly gather the net to
fit around the bear's waist. Secure the thread
firmly to ensure the skirt remains gathered.
Using pink crochet cotton, work a row of sc (UK
dc) along the top edge of the skirt, working
through both thicknesses of net.
Turn, and work a further row of sc (UK dc).
Fasten off.

Head dress

Using metallic yarn, make 4 ch, join in a circle
with a sl st.
Next row: *4 ch, 1 sc (UK dc) in circle*, rep from
* to * 5 times, join with a sl st to beg of row.
Fasten off.

To make up

Make the wand by wrapping the cocktail stick
tightly with a length of metallic yarn, leaving a
small section at one end uncovered to enable
you to stick on the star. Secure the ends of the
yarn with craft glue. Take two adhesive stars
and press them together firmly, one on each
side of the top of the stick. Secure the wand
in the bear's paw by threading it through the
crochet stitches. Sew the wings together firmly
at the centre. Place them in the middle of the
bear's back and secure. Sew small sequin stars
randomly over the net skirt. Place the skirt
around the bear's waist and sew the crochet
band together at the centre back. Finally, work
in the ends of the crocheted head dress and
attach an adhesive star firmly to the centre. Sew
the head dress to the top of the bear's head
with some tiny stitches.

Mazzy the Keep-fit Bear

Materials and equipment:

Crochet hook size 2.50mm (US B-1, UK 13)

No. 5 crochet cotton – 1 ball of beige

Small amount of crochet cotton in ecru, black, lilac and dark pink

Toy stuffing

Black floss for embroidering features

Sewing needle and threads in colours to match crochet cotton

Instructions:

Make the bear following the basic instructions at the beginning of the book, using beige for the head and legs, lilac for the body and ecru for the muzzle and ears. For each arm, work the first 10 rows in beige, then change to lilac and complete the rest of the arm.

Leg warmers (make 2)

Row 1: using dark pink, make 18 ch, 1 dc (*UK tr*) in 3rd ch from hook, 1 dc (*UK tr*) in each ch to end, turn.
Row 2: 3 ch, miss 1 dc (*UK tr*), 1 dc (*UK tr*) in each dc (*UK tr*) to end.
Row 3: rep row 2.
Row 4: 1 ch, 1 sc (*UK dc*) in each dc (*UK tr*) to end. Fasten off.

Head band

Using dark pink, make 30 ch, break pink and join in lilac, work 1 sc (*UK dc*) in 2nd ch from hook, 1 sc (*UK dc*) in each ch to end, break lilac and turn.
Join in dark pink, sl st in each sc (*UK dc*) to end. Fasten off.

Sports bag, front and back

Row 1: using dark pink, make 13 ch, 1 sc (*UK dc*) in 2nd ch from hook, 1 sc (*UK dc*) in each ch to end, turn.
Row 2: 1 ch, 1 sc (*UK dc*) in each sc (*UK dc*) to end, turn.
Repeat row 2 18 times. Fasten off.

Bag handles (make 2)

Using black, make 18 ch. Fasten off.

Bag strap

Using black, make 38 ch. Fasten off.

Arm bands (make 2)

Using dark pink, make 18 ch. Fasten off.

Neck band

Using dark pink, make 30 ch. Fasten off.

To make up

Sew the arm bands on to the arms, where the colour changes from beige to lilac. Arrange the neck band around the bear's neck so that it is scooped slightly at the front, and attach it to the body with one or two small stitches. Join in the head band in a circle and place it on the bear's head. Secure with a few tiny stitches. Take the main piece of the sports bag, fold it in half and sew the side seams. Stuff it lightly with a little stuffing to give it shape and close the top. Sew a handle to either side of the bag and attach the strap at either end. Fold the leg warmers in half lengthways and sew the side seam. Slip them on to the bear's legs.

Belinda Butterfly Bear

Materials and equipment:

Crochet hook size 2.50mm (US B-1, UK 13)

No. 5 crochet cotton – 1 ball of white

Small amounts of crochet cotton in beige, dark brown and light blue

Black and yellow floss for embroidering features and butterfly

Tiny paper flowers in yellow and pink

Tiny pale blue ribbon bow

Toy stuffing

Sewing needle and threads in colours to match crochet cotton

Instructions:

Make the bear following the basic instructions at the beginning of the book, using white for the head, body, arms and legs and beige for the muzzle and ears.

Skirt

Row 1: using light blue, make 30 ch, join with a sl st to beg of row, making sure you do not twist the chain.
Row 2: 1 ch, 1 sc (UK dc) in each ch to end, joining as before.
Row 3: 4 ch, miss 2 sc (UK dc), 1 sc (UK dc) in next sc (UK dc), *2 ch, miss 2 ch, 1 sc (UK dc) in next sc (UK dc)*, rep from * to * all round, 2 ch, sl st to 2nd of 4 turning ch of previous row.
Row 4: *3 ch, 1 sc (UK dc) in next 3 ch loop*, rep from * to * all round, joining as before.
Row 5: as row 4.
Row 6: [1 sc (UK dc), 2 dc (UK tr), 1 sc (UK dc)] in each 3 ch loop. Join with a sl st to beg of row. Fasten off.

Basket

Row 1: using dark brown, make 3 ch, 14 dc (UK tr) in 2nd ch from hook, join with a sl st.
Row 2: 2 dc (UK tr) in each dc (UK tr) all round. Join as before.
Row 3: working into back loop of stitch only, 1 dc (UK tr) in each st to end, join as before. Work 2 rows of sc (UK dc). Fasten off.

Basket handle

Using dark brown, make 20 ch, 1 sc (UK dc) in 2nd ch from hook, 1 sc (UK dc) in each ch to end. Fasten off.

Butterfly

Using light blue, make 2 ch, 3 dc (UK tr) in 2nd ch from hook, 1 sl st in same place, 3 ch, 3 dc (UK tr) in same place, 1 sl st in same place, 3 ch, 3 dc (UK tr) in same place, sl st in same place, 3 ch, 3 dc (UK tr) in same place, sl st in same place and fasten off. Sew the centre together to form four wings.

To make up

Work in the ends on all the pieces. Attach the tiny blue ribbon bow to the bear's head. Slip the skirt on to the bear with the join at the centre back. Add a tiny amount of stuffing to the basket to give it a rounded shape and sew one end of the handle on to each side. Wire the flowers together into a neat bunch, place them inside the basket and secure them with a few a stitches. Shape the butterfly's wings, then take some yellow floss and sew a tiny spot on to each wing using French knots. Use some black floss to work the body in straight stitches. Fray the end of the black floss to make antennae. Sew the butterfly to the bear's paw.

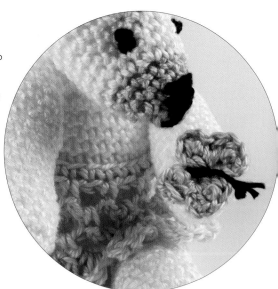

Anthony Garden Bear

Materials and equipment:

Crochet hook size 2.50mm (US B-1, UK 13)

No. 5 crochet cotton – 1 ball of beige and 1 ball of mid green

Small amounts of crochet cotton in dark brown, mid brown, light blue and dark green

Black floss for embroidering features

Small amount of metallic yarn in silver

2 tiny plastic flowers

Tiny card fork and trowel

Toy stuffing

Sewing needle and threads in colours to match crochet cotton

Instructions:

Make the bear following the basic instructions at the beginning of the book, using beige for the head, body and arms and dark brown for the muzzle and ears. For the legs, work using mid green, then join in light blue at row 8 and work rows 8, 10 and 12 in light blue.

Apron

Row 1: using mid green, make 17 ch, 1 dc (UK tr) in 4th ch from hook, 1dc (UK tr) in each ch to end, turn.
Row 2: 1 ch, 1 sc (UK dc) in each sc (UK dc) to end, turn.
Row 3: 3 ch, miss 1 dc (UK tr), 1 dc (UK tr) in each dc (UK tr) to end.

Row 4: 1 ch, 1 sc (UK dc) in each dc (UK tr) to end, turn.
Rows 5 and 6: rep rows 3 and 4.
Row 7: sl st over 4 dc (UK tr), 3 ch, 1 dc (UK tr) in each st to last 3 dc (UK tr), turn.
Row 8: 3 ch, dc (UK tr) 2 tog, work to last 3 sts, dc (UK tr) 2 tog, 1 dc (UK tr) in top of turning ch of previous row.

Pocket

Row 1: using dark green, make 10 ch, 1 sc (UK dc) in 2nd ch from hook, 1 sc (UK dc) in each ch to end, turn.
Row 2: 1 ch, 1 sc (UK dc) in each sc (UK dc) to end, turn.
Rows 3 and 4: rep row 2. Fasten off.

Spade – blade

Row 1: using metallic yarn, make 7 ch, 1 sc (UK dc) in 2nd ch from hook, 1 sc (UK dc) in each ch to end, turn.
Row 2: 1 ch, 1 sc (UK dc) in each sc (UK dc) to end, turn.
Repeat last row 12 times. Fasten off.

Spade – shaft

Row 1: using dark brown, make 12 ch, 1 sc (UK dc) in 2nd ch from hook, 1 sc (UK dc) in each ch to end, turn.
Row 2: 1 ch, 1 sc (UK dc) in each sc (UK dc) to end, turn.
Row 3: rep row 2. Fasten off.

Spade – handle

Row 1: using dark brown, make 8 ch, 1 sc (UK dc) in 2nd ch from hook, 1 sc (UK dc) in each ch to end, turn.
Row 2: 1 ch, 1 sc (UK dc) in each sc (UK dc) to end, turn.
Row 3: rep row 2. Fasten off.

Flower pot

Row 1: using dark brown, make 2 ch, 6 sc (UK dc) in 2nd ch from hook, join in a circle with a sl st.
Row 2: 1 ch, 2 sc (UK dc) in each sc (UK dc) all round, join as before.
Rows 3–7: 1 ch, 1 sc (UK dc) in each st, join as before.

Soil for pot

Using dark brown, make 3 ch, 6 sc (*UK dc*) in 2nd ch from hook, join in a circle. Work 2 sc (*UK dc*) in each st all round, join and fasten off.

To make up

Work in the ends on all the pieces. Sew the pocket to the front of the apron. Using green yarn, make a chain long enough to go round the bear's neck, then attach the top of the apron at each corner. Make two short lengths of chain as ties for the apron and attach one on each side. Put the apron on to the bear and tie the apron at the back. Fold the blade part of the spade in half lengthwise and stitch the sides together. Fold the shaft lengthways into a tight oblong and stitch it firmly. Do the same with the handle. Stitch the handle to the shaft, then attach the shaft to the blade. Lightly stuff the flower pot to give it shape. Put the soil inside the pot and catch it in place. Push the two plastic flowers through the centre of the soil and secure with a few stitches. Stitch the fork and trowel on to the pocket.

Caroline in the Kitchen

Materials and equipment:

Crochet hook size 2.50mm (US B-1, UK 13)

No. 5 crochet cotton – 1 ball of yellow

Small amounts of crochet cotton in mid brown, dark brown, light beige, green, pale pink and mid pink

Black floss for embroidering features

Toy stuffing

Sewing needle and threads in colours to match crochet cotton

Instructions:

Make the bear following the basic instructions at the beginning of the book, using yellow for the head, body, arms and legs and mid brown for the muzzle and ears.

Apron

Row 1: using pale pink, make 15 ch, 1 dc (*UK tr*) in 4th ch from hook, 1 dc (*UK tr*) in each ch to end, turn.
Row 2: 1 ch, 1 sc (*UK dc*) in each sc (*UK dc*) to end, turn.
Row 3: 3 ch, miss 1 dc (*UK tr*), 1 dc (*UK tr*) in each dc (*UK tr*) to end.
Row 4: 1 ch, 1 sc (*UK dc*) in each dc (*UK tr*) to end, turn.
Rows 5 and 6: rep rows 3 and 4.
Row 7: sl st over 4 dc (*UK tr*), 3 ch, 1 dc (*UK tr*) in each st to last 3 dc (*UK tr*), turn.

Shape waist:
Row 8: 3 ch, dc (*UK tr*) 2 tog, work to last 3 sts, dc (*UK tr*) 2 tog, 1 dc (*UK tr*) in top of turning ch of previous row.
Row 9: sc (*UK dc*) 2 tog, work to last 2 sts, sc (*UK dc*) 2 tog, turn.
Row 10: 1 sc (*UK dc*) in each of next 3 sts, turn.
Work the strap:
Row 11: 1 sc (*UK dc*) in next st, sc (*UK dc*) 2 tog, turn.
Work in sc (*UK dc*) on these 2 sts until strap is long enough to go round bear's neck and will reach to the other corner of the apron bib. Fasten off.

Apron edging

Row 1: using mid pink, join yarn to one side of waist. Work sc (*UK dc*) all round apron to other side of waist, turn.
Row 2: 1 ch, *1 sc (*UK dc*) in next st, 1 dc (*UK tr*) in next st*, rep from * to * all round edge. Fasten off.

Apron ties (make 2)

Row 1: using pale pink, make 17 ch, 1 sc (*UK dc*) in 2nd ch from hook, 1 sc (*UK dc*) in each ch to end, turn.
Row 2: 1 ch, 1 sc (*UK dc*) in each st to end. Fasten off.

Pocket

Row 1: using mid pink, make 8 ch, 1 sc (*UK dc*) in 2nd ch from hook, 1 sc (*UK dc*) in each ch to end, turn.
Row 2: 1 ch, 1 sc (*UK dc*) in each sc (*UK dc*) to end, turn.
Rows 3 and 4: rep row 2. Fasten off.

Basket

Row 1: using dark brown, make 3 ch, 14 dc (*UK tr*) in 2nd ch from hook, join with a sl st.
Row 2: 2 dc (*UK tr*) in each dc (*UK tr*) all round, join as before.
Row 3: working into back loop of st only, work 1 dc (*UK tr*) into each dc (*UK tr*) to end, join.
Work 2 rows of sc (*UK dc*). Fasten off.

Handles (make 2)

Using dark brown, make 10 ch. Fasten off.

Apples (make 5)
Using green, make 3 ch, work 9 dc (UK tr) in 2nd ch from hook, break yarn and run end through each st.

Pie top
Row 1: using light beige, make 2 ch, 6 sc (UK dc) in 2nd ch from hook, join in a circle with a sl st.
Row 2: 1 ch, 2 sc (UK dc) in each st to end, join as before.
Row 3: 1 ch, [1 sc (UK dc) in next st, 2 sc (UK dc) in next st] to end, join.
Row 4: 1 ch, [1 sc (UK dc) in each of next 2 sts, 2 sc (UK dc) in next st] to end, join.
Row 5: 1 ch, [1 sc (UK dc) in each of next 3 sts, 2 sc (UK dc) in next st] to end, join.
Row 6: 1 ch, *1 dc (UK tr) in next st, 1 sc (UK dc) in next st*, rep from * to * all round, join with a sl st. Fasten off.

Pie base
Work as for pie top, but omit the last row.

To make up
Work in the ends on all the pieces. Sew the top of the pie to the base, adding a tiny piece of stuffing as you do so. Shape it into a pie shape. For each leaf on top of the pie, use light beige to make 5 ch. Form each chain into a tiny loop and sew them to the centre of the pie top. To make the apron, work in the ends on all the pieces. Sew the pocket to the centre front of the apron and attach one tie to each side at the waist. Put the apron on to the bear, pass the strap round the bear's neck and stitch it in place to the other side of the bib. Sew the handles to the sides of the basket. Draw the green chains up to form tight balls, adding a tiny piece of stuffing as you do so, close and secure. Thread a short length of dark brown through the top of each apple to make a stalk. Place the apples inside the basket.

Roz the Artist Bear

Materials and equipment:

Crochet hook size 2.50mm (US B-1, UK 13)

No. 5 crochet cotton – 1 ball of pale yellow and 1 ball of light blue

Small amounts of crochet cotton in mid brown, dark brown, beige, navy blue (no. 3) and white

Dark brown floss for embroidering features, and green and yellow floss for embroidery on easel

Tiny coloured beads for paint palette

6 cocktail sticks, 5 with one blunt end and 1 with two blunt ends.

Toy stuffing

Sewing needle and threads in colours to match crochet cotton

Instructions:

Make the bear following the basic instructions at the beginning of the book, using pale yellow for the head, body, arms and legs, dark brown for the ears and beige for the muzzle.

Sleeves (make 2)

Row 1: using light blue, make 17 ch, 1 dc (UK tr) in 3rd ch from hook, 1 dc (UK tr) in each ch to end, turn.
Row 2: 3 ch, miss 1 st, 1 dc (UK tr) in each st to end.
Rows 3 and 4: rep row 2.
Row 5: 1 ch, 1 sc (UK dc) in each st to end. Fasten off.

Smock (make 2)

Row 1: using light blue, make 20 ch, 1 dc (UK tr) in 3rd ch from hook, 1 dc (UK tr) in each ch to end, turn.
Row 2: 3 ch, miss 1 st, 1 dc (UK tr) in each dc (UK tr) to end.
Row 3: 3 ch, miss 1 st, dc (UK tr) 2 tog, dc (UK tr) to last 3 sts, dc (UK tr) 2 tog, 1 dc (UK tr) in last st.
Row 4: sl st across next 4 dc (UK tr), 3 ch, 1 dc (UK tr) in each dc (UK tr) to last 3 dc (UK tr), turn.
Row 5: 3 ch, 1 dc (UK tr) in each st to end.
Row 6: 3 ch, 1 dc (UK tr), 1 hdc (UK htr), 5 sc (UK dc), 1hdc (UK htr), 2 dc (UK tr). Fasten off.

Beret

Row 1: using navy blue, make 30 ch, 1 sc (UK dc) in 2nd ch from hook, 1 sc (UK dc) in each ch to end, join with a sl st into a circle.
Rows 2 and 3: sc (UK dc) all round, join as before.
Row 4: 1 ch, *1 sc (UK dc) in next sc (UK dc), 2 sc (UK dc) in next sc (UK dc)*, rep from * to * all round, join as before.
Rows 5 and 6: sc (UK dc) all round, join as before.
Row 7: 1 ch, *sc (UK dc) 2 tog, 1 sc (UK dc) in next st*, rep from * to * all round, ending last rep sc (UK dc) 2 tog, join as before.
Row 8: sc (UK dc) all round.
Row 9: 1 ch, *sc (UK dc) 2 tog, 1 sc (UK dc) in next st*, rep from * to * all round, ending last rep sc (UK dc) 2 tog, join as before.
Row 10: sc (UK dc) all round.
Row 11: 1 ch, *sc (UK dc) 2 tog, 1 sc (UK dc) in next st*, rep from * to * all round, ending last rep 1 sc (UK dc) in each of last 2 sts, join as before.
Row 12: sc (UK dc) all round.
Break yarn and run the thread through each sc (UK dc) all round. Draw up and fasten off. Make a tiny loop and attach to the top of the beret.

Easel

Using mid brown, make a ch the same length as a cocktail stick.
Work 3 rows of sc (UK dc) on this chain, fasten off. Wrap the crochet piece lengthways around

the stick and oversew it in place firmly. The point should be visible at one end. Repeat this on a further three cocktail sticks, including the one with two blunt ends.

Canvas
Row 1: using white, make 15 ch, 1 sc (*UK dc*) in 2nd ch from hook, 1 sc (*UK dc*) in each ch to end, turn.
Rows 2–14: 1 ch, 1 sc (*UK dc*) in each ch to end, turn.
Fasten off.
Embroider a flower on to the front of the canvas using yellow and green floss.

Palette
Row 1: using white, make 9 ch, 1 sc (*UK dc*) in 2nd ch from hook, 1 sc (*UK dc*) in each ch to end, turn.
Rows 2–6: 1 ch, 1 sc (*UK dc*) in each ch to end. Do not fasten off but continue along 1 short end as follows:
Row 7: 1 sc (*UK dc*) in next 2 row ends, 2 ch, miss 2 row ends, 1 sc (*UK dc*) in last 2 row ends, turn.
Row 8: 1 ch, sc (*UK dc*) to end, working 2 sc (*UK dc*) in space made on previous row. Fasten off.

Take 8 different coloured beads and sew in place on the palette to represent paint colours.

To make up
Work in the ends on all the pieces. Catch the back and front smock pieces at the shoulder edges, just enough to hold them together. Stitch the sleeves in place. Sew the side and sleeve seams. Put the smock on to the bear and sew the shoulder seams on either side. Place the beret on the side of the bear's head and secure with a few stitches. Place the palette on the bear's paw and stitch it in place. Take two cocktail sticks and flatten the sharp end of each slightly to split the wood and create a brush effect. Place the brushes into the thumb hole on the palette and secure with some tiny stitches. Now assemble the easel. First make an A frame by stitching together the top part of two sticks, then sew the stick with two blunt ends horizontally across the centre to create the 'A'. Secure a fourth stick at the back of the frame so that the easel will stand up. Oversew the top of the three upright sticks together firmly. Place the canvas centrally on to the cross bar of the easel and sew it in place.

Musical Briony Bear

Materials and equipment:

Crochet hook size 2.50mm (US B-1, UK 13)

No. 5 crochet cotton – 1 ball of beige

Small amounts of crochet cotton in mid brown, dark brown, red, black, white and green

Black floss for embroidering features, yellow floss for flower centre and white floss for embroidery on accordion

Toy stuffing

Sewing needle and threads in colours to match crochet cotton

Instructions:

Make the bear following the basic instructions at the beginning of the book, using beige for the head, body, arms and legs and mid brown for the muzzle and ears.

Accordion – bellows

Row 1: using black, make 18 ch, 1 sc (UK dc) in 2nd ch from hook, 1 sc (UK dc) in each ch to end, turn.

Row 2: 1 ch, 1 sc (UK dc) in each st to end, working into back loops only.

Rep row 2 until you have 6 ridges on either side. Fasten off.

Accordion – button section

Row 1: using red, make 9 ch, work 1 sc (UK dc) into 2nd ch from hook, 1 sc (UK dc) in each ch to end, turn.

Rows 2–10: 1 ch, 1 sc (UK dc) in each st to end, turn.

Fasten off.

Accordion – keyboard section

Work in two parts – one as the button section (above), and the other in the same way but repeating row 10 twice before fastening off. For the keys, use white to make 3 ch, 1 sc (UK dc) in 2nd ch from hook, 1 sc (UK dc) in last st, turn and work sc (UK dc) on these 2 sts for a further 8 rows. Fasten off.

Strap

Using brown make 18 ch. Fasten off.

Flower

Using red, make 3 ch and join into a circle with a sl st. *3 ch, 1 sc (UK dc) in circle*, rep from * to * 5 times. Fasten off.

Leaf

Using green, make 5 ch, 1 sc (UK dc) in 2nd ch from hook, 1 hdc (UK htr) in each of next 2 ch, 1 sc (UK dc) in last ch. Work along other side of starting ch in same way, join with a sl st.

Collar

Row 1: using white, make 25 ch, work 1 sc (UK dc) in 2nd ch from hook, 1 sc (UK dc) in each ch to end, turn.

Row 2: 4 ch, miss 2 sts, 1 sc (UK dc) in next st, *2 ch, miss 2 sts, 1 sc (UK dc) in next st*, rep from * to * to end.

Row 3: 1 ch, *2 sc (UK dc) in first st, sl st in next sc (UK dc)*, rep from * to * ending last rep, sl st in top of turning ch of previous row. Fasten off.

To make up

Work in the ends on all the pieces. Place the collar around the bear's neck, with the opening at the centre front, and stitch it in place. Sew a French knot into the centre of the flower using yellow floss. Attach the flower to the leaf and stitch them on the bear's head beside one ear. The accordion is assembled in three pieces. Take the button section and fold it

lengthwise into a tight oblong. Sew along the sides. Embroider eight tiny French knots on to one side using white floss (follow the picture opposite for guidance). For the keyboard section, fold both parts into tight oblongs and place one behind the other so that the longer part sits at the back – from the side, it will have an L shape. Sew these parts together. Take the keys and sew them on to one side (again, refer to the photograph). Use black floss to embroider on the black keys. Take the bellows section and fold it in half so that the ridges are vertical. Sew along the two short ends and base, putting a tiny amount of stuffing into the piece before closing. Attach the keyboard and button sections to the bellows. Attach a strap to the buttons end of the accordion and place it over the bear's arm.

Bernie the Christmas Elf

Materials and equipment:

Crochet hook size 2.50mm (US B-1, UK 13)

No. 5 crochet cotton – 1 ball of beige and 1 ball of red

Small amounts of crochet cotton in dark brown and mid green

Black floss for embroidering features

3 tiny gold beads for hat

Toy stuffing

Sewing needle and threads in colours to match crochet cotton

Instructions:

Make the bear following the basic instructions at the beginning of the book, using beige for the head, body, arms and legs and dark brown for the muzzle and ears.

Sleeves

Row 1: using red, make 17 ch, 1 dc (*UK tr*) in 3rd ch from hook, 1 dc (*UK tr*) in each ch to end, turn.
Rows 2–4: 3 ch, miss 1 st, 1 dc (*UK tr*) in each st to end.
Row 5: 1 ch, 1 sc (*UK dc*) in each st to end. Fasten off.

Tunic (make 2)

Row 1: using red, make 20 ch, dc (*UK tr*) in 3rd ch from hook, 1 dc (*UK tr*) in each ch to end, turn.
Rows 2 and 3: 3 ch, miss 1 st, 1 dc (*UK tr*) in each dc (*UK tr*) to end.
Row 4: 3 ch, miss 1 st, dc (*UK tr*) 2 tog, dc (*UK tr*) to last 3 sts, dc (*UK tr*) 2 tog, 1 dc (*UK tr*) in last st.
Row 5: sl st across next 4 dc (*UK tr*), 3 ch, 1 dc (*UK tr*) in each dc (*UK tr*) to last 3 dc (*UK tr*), turn.
Row 6: 3 ch, dc (*UK tr*) in each st to end.
Row 7: 3 ch, 1 dc (*UK tr*), 1 hdc (*UK htr*), 5 sc (*UK dc*), 1 hdc (*UK htr*), 2 dc (*UK tr*). Fasten off.

Collar

Using green, make 24 ch, 1 sc (*UK dc*) in 2nd ch from hook, dc (*UK tr*) 2 tog over next 2 ch. Fasten off.
*Rejoin yarn to next ch, dc (*UK tr*) 2 tog over next 2 ch. Fasten off.* Rep from * to * along rest of ch, ending 1 sc (*UK dc*) in last ch.

Hat

Row 1: using green, make 26 ch, 1 sc (*UK dc*) in 2nd ch from hook, 1 sc (*UK dc*) in each ch to end, turn.
Row 2: 1 ch, 1 sc (*UK dc*) in each st to end, turn.
Rows 3 and 4: changing to red, 3 ch, miss 1 st, 1 dc (*UK tr*) in each st to end, turn.
Rows 5 and 6: 3 ch, miss 1 st, dc (*UK tr*) 2 tog across row to last st, 1 dc (*UK tr*) in last st, turn.
Rows 7 and 8: 3 ch, 1 dc (*UK tr*) in each st to end.
Row 9: 3 ch, dc (*UK tr*) 2 tog 3 times, 1 dc (*UK tr*) in last tr, turn.
Row 10: 3 ch, miss 1 dc (*UK tr*), 1 dc (*UK tr*) in each st to end. Break yarn.
Run thread through last row, draw up and secure.

Belt

Using green, make ch long enough to go round the bear's waist with a little extra for overlap. Fasten off.

To make up

Work in the ends on all the pieces. Catch the back and front tunic pieces at the shoulder edges to hold them in place. Stitch the sleeves in place. Sew the side and sleeve seams and put the tunic on to the bear. Sew the shoulder seams on either side. Sew the seam on the hat and attach three tiny gold beads to the point. Place the belt around the bear's waist and catch the ends together at the centre back. Place the collar around the bear's neck and join at the centre back. Stretch it slightly to give a good fit.

Paul the Panda Bear

Materials and equipment:

Crochet hook size 2.50mm (US B-1, UK 13)

No. 5 crochet cotton – 1 ball of black and 1 ball of white

Small amounts of crochet cotton in mid brown and mid green

Black floss for embroidering features

Toy stuffing

Sewing needle and threads in colours to match crochet cotton

Instructions:

Make the bear following the basic instructions at the beginning of the book, using black for the ears, arms and legs and white for the head. For the body, work the first 9 rows in white and the remainder in black.

Eye patches (make 2)
Row 1: using black, make 2 ch, 6 sc (*UK dc*) in 2nd ch from hook, join in a circle with a sl st.
Row 2: 2 sc (*UK dc*) in each sc (*UK dc*) all round, join with a sl st.
Row 3: 1 sc (*UK dc*) in each of next 4 sc (*UK dc*). Fasten off.

Bamboo shoot
Row 1: using brown, make 12 ch, 1 sc (*UK dc*) in 2nd ch from hook, 1 sc (*UK dc*) in each ch to end, turn.
Row 2: sc (*UK dc*) to end. Fasten off.

Green leaves (make 3)
Using green, make 5 ch. Fasten off.

To make up
Work in the ends on all the pieces, leaving a long tail on the end of each leaf. Place the eye patches on either side of the head, pull them into an oval shape and sew in place. Using black floss, make a French knot in the centre of each eye patch to make the eyes. Fold the brown section of the bamboo in half lengthways and sew it together firmly. Take a leaf strand and run the long thread down into the top of the brown stem. Secure it with one or two tiny stitches. Repeat with the remaining leaves. Sew the bamboo shoot to the palm of the panda's paw, and catch the other paw to the shoot to look as though the panda is holding it.

Juan the Flamenco Bear

Materials and equipment:

Crochet hook size 2.50mm (US B-1, UK 13)

No. 5 crochet cotton – 1 ball of beige

Small amounts of crochet cotton in black, red, dark brown, mid brown, green and white

Black floss for embroidering features

Toy stuffing

Sewing needle and threads in colours to match crochet cotton

Instructions:

Make the bear following the basic instructions at the beginning of the book, using beige for the head, body, arms and legs and dark brown for the muzzle and ears.

Hat

Row 1: using black, make 2 ch, 6 sc (UK dc) in 2nd ch from hook, join this row and all subsequent rows with a sl st to form a circle.

Row 2: 2 sc (UK dc) in each sc (UK dc) all round [12 sts].

Row 3: inc 4 sc (UK dc) evenly all round [16 sts].

Rows 4–7: sc (UK dc) all round.

Row 8: 2 sc (UK dc) in each sc (UK dc) to end [32 sts].

Rows 9 and 10: sc (UK dc), inc 6 sts evenly on each row [44 sts].

Row 11: sc (UK dc).

Row 12: 1 sl st in each st round brim. Join and fasten off.

Hat band

Using red, make a chain long enough to fit around the crown of the hat. Work 1 row of sc (UK dc) along the chain. Fasten off.

Bandana

Row 1: using red, make 2 ch, 2 sc (UK dc) in 2nd ch from hook, turn.

Row 2: 1 ch, 1 sc (UK dc) in each st to end, turn.

Rows 3–7: sc (UK dc), inc 1 st at each end of row until there are 12 sc (UK dc).

Row 8: work 1 sc (UK dc) in each of next 2 sts, turn.

Rows 9–16: continue in sc (UK dc) on these 2 sts. Fasten off.

Miss centre 8 sts, rejoin yarn and complete to match other side.

Guitar – neck

Row 1: using mid brown, make 15 ch, work 1 sc (UK dc) in 2nd ch from hook, 1 sc (UK dc) in each ch to end, turn.

Rows 2 and 3: sc (UK dc). Fasten off.

Guitar – body, top section (make 2)

Row 1: using mid brown, make 2 ch, 6 sc (UK dc) in 2nd ch from hook, join with a sl st.

Row 2: 2 sc (UK dc) in each sc (UK dc) all round, join with a sl st. Fasten off.

Guitar – body, bottom section (make 2)

Work as top section to end of row 2.

Row 3: *1 sc (UK dc) in next st, 2 sc (UK dc) in next st*, rep from * to * all round. Fasten off.

Guitar – side

Using dark brown, make a ch long enough to fit all round the outside edge of the guitar body. Work 1 dc (UK tr) in 3rd ch from hook, 1 dc (UK tr) in each ch to end. Fasten off.

Rose

Using red, make 3 ch, join into a circle with a sl st.

Work *3 ch, 1 sc (UK dc) into circle*, rep from * to * 5 times. Fasten off.

Gather the base of the flower to form a rose.

Rose stem

Using green, make 7 ch to form the stem. Thread green into a needle and work two loops on either side of stem to form tiny leaves.

To make up

Work in the ends on all the pieces. Sew the hat band around the hat. Place the hat on to the bear's head, position it at an angle and sew it in place. Using white yarn, embroider French knots all over the bandana in random spots. Tie the bandana around the bear's neck. Fold the guitar neck lengthwise into a neat oblong and oversew it firmly together. For the guitar body, sew one top and one bottom section together for the front, and repeat for the back. Carefully pin the side of the guitar around the outer edge of either the front or back of the body, then sew it in place. Take the other part of the guitar body and stitch this to the side in the same way, leaving a small opening at the top. Push a small amount of stuffing into the guitar body, shape it, then insert the neck into the opening and secure with a few stitches. Using black yarn, sew lengths of thread on to the front of the guitar to represent strings. Secure them at the top and bottom. Make two French knots on each side of the head to represent the pegs. To finish, attach the stem to the rose and pull the stem through the bear's muzzle using a crochet hook.

Sophie the Swimmer

Materials and equipment:

Crochet hook size 2.50mm (US B-1, UK 13)

No. 5 crochet cotton – 1 ball of pale yellow

Small amounts of crochet cotton in black, beige, blue and white

Black floss for embroidering features

Toy stuffing

Sewing needle and threads in colours to match crochet cotton

Instructions:

Make the bear following the basic instructions at the beginning of the book, using pale yellow for the head, body, arms and legs and beige for the muzzle and ears.

Swimsuit

Row 1: using black, make 11 ch, 1 sc (UK dc) in 2nd ch from hook, 1 sc (UK dc) in each ch to end, turn.

Rows 2 and 3: 1 ch, 1 sc (UK dc) in each sc (UK dc) to end, turn.

Rows 4–6: inc 1 sc (UK dc) at each end of row until there are 16 sc (UK dc).

Rows 7–9: sc (UK dc).

Row 10: sl st over 3 sc (UK dc), sc (UK dc) to last 3 sc (UK dc), turn.

Row 11: sc (UK dc).

Rows 12–13: dec 1 sc (UK dc) each end of row until there are 6 sc (UK dc).

Rows 14–21: work 8 rows sc (UK dc).

Rows 22–23: inc 1 sc (UK dc) at each end of row until there are 10 sc (UK dc).

Row 24: sc (UK dc) to end, make 4 ch, turn.

Row 25: 1 sc (UK dc) in 2nd ch from hook, 1 sc (UK dc) in each sc (UK dc) to end, make 4 ch, turn.

Row 26: repeat row 25.

Rows 27–29: sc (UK dc).

Rows 30–32: dec 1 sc (UK dc) at each end of row until there are 10 sc (UK dc).

Rows 33–34: work in sc (UK dc).

Row 35: 2 sc (UK dc), turn.

Work in sc (UK dc) on these 2 sts until strap is long enough to fit over bear's shoulder to back of swimsuit. Fasten off.

Miss centre 6 sc (UK dc), rejoin yarn to rem 2 sts and work to match other strap. Fasten off.

Towel

Row 1: using white, make 15 ch, 1 sc (UK dc) in 2nd ch from hook, 1 sc (UK dc) in each ch to end, turn.

Row 2: 1 hdc (UK htr) in each st to end, turn.

Rows 3 and 4: join in blue and work sc (UK dc).

Rows 5 and 6: pick up white and work hdc (UK htr).

Rows 7 and 8: pick up blue and work sc (UK dc).

Row 9: pick up white and work hdc (UK htr).

Row 10: sc (UK dc). Fasten off.

To make up

Work in the ends on all the pieces. Sew up the side seams of the swimsuit and slip it on to the bear. Take the straps over the bear's shoulders and sew them on to either side of the costume at the back. Embroider a tiny motif in white on the front.

Ali the Baby Bear

Materials and equipment:

Crochet hook size 2.50mm (US B-1, UK 13)

No. 5 crochet cotton – 1 ball of pale pink

Small amounts of crochet cotton in white and salmon pink

Small amount of no. 3 crochet cotton in mid pink for clothes

3 pale pink ribbon-and-rose bows

Tiny pink safety pin

Brown floss for embroidering features

Toy stuffing

Sewing needle and threads in colours to match crochet cotton

Instructions:

Make the bear following the basic instructions at the beginning of the book, using pale pink for the head, body, arms and legs and salmon pink for the muzzle and ears.

Bootees (make 2)

Row 1: using mid pink, make 8 ch, 1 dc (*UK tr*) in 2nd ch from hook, 1 dc (*UK tr*) in each st to last ch, 5 dc (*UK tr*) in last ch, do not turn. Continue along other side of starting ch. Work 1 dc (*UK tr*) in each st to last ch, 4 dc (*UK tr*) in last ch, join with a sl st to beg of row. This completes the sole.
Rows 2 and 3: 2 ch, 1dc (*UK tr*) in each dc (*UK tr*) all round, join with a sl st to beg of row.
Row 4: sc (*UK dc*).
Row 5: 3 ch, miss 1 sc (*UK dc*), 1 dc (*UK tr*) in next sc (*UK dc*), *1 ch, miss 2 sc (*UK dc*), 1 dc (*UK tr*) in next sc (*UK dc*)*, rep from * to * to end of row, sl st into beg of row.
Row 6: 3 ch, 2 dc (*UK tr*) in first ch sp, 1 sc (*UK dc*) in next ch sp, *3 dc (*UK tr*) in next ch sp, 1 sc (*UK dc*) in next ch sp*, rep from * to * all round, join to base of first dc (*UK tr*) at beg of row. Fasten off.

Diaper/nappy

Row 1: using white yarn, make 36 ch, 1 sc (*UK dc*) in 2nd ch from hook, 1 sc (*UK dc*) in each ch to end, turn.
Row 2: 1 ch, 1 sc (*UK dc*) in each ch to end, turn.
Rows 3–17: dec 1 sc (*UK dc*) at each end of row until 1 sc (*UK dc*) rem. Fasten off.

Top

Row 1: using mid pink, make 32 ch, 1 sc (*UK dc*) in 2nd ch from hook, 1 sc (*UK dc*) in each ch to end.
Row 2: 4 ch, miss 2 sc (*UK dc*), 1 dc (*UK tr*) in next st, *1 ch, miss 1 sc (*UK dc*), 1 dc (*UK tr*) in next st*, rep from * to * to end. Fasten off.

For left back, work along starting ch as follows:
Row 1: 1 sc (*UK dc*) in each of next 6 ch, turn.
Row 2: sc (*UK dc*) 2 tog, sc (*UK dc*) to end, turn.
Rows 3–5: sc (*UK dc*).
Row 6: 3 sc (*UK dc*), turn.
Rows 7–9: sc (*UK dc*). Fasten off.

Return to main piece and continue working along starting ch for front.
Row 1: miss 3 ch, join yarn to next ch, work 1 sc (*UK dc*) in same place as join, 1 sc (*UK dc*) in each of next 13 ch [14 sts].

Row 2: sc (UK dc) 2 tog, sc (UK dc) to last 2 sts, sc (UK dc) 2 tog.
Rows 3–5: sc (UK dc).

Shape neck:
Row 6: work across 3 sc (UK dc), turn.
Rows 7–9: sc (UK dc). Fasten off.

Miss centre 6 sc (UK dc), rejoin yarn to next sc (UK dc), 1 sc (UK dc) in next 3 sc (UK dc), turn and complete right back to match left back, reversing shaping instructions. Fasten off. Work to match first side of neck. Fasten off. Join shoulder seams.

Work edging along bottom:
Join yarn to top of first dc (UK tr), 3 ch, 2 dc

(UK tr) in first ch sp, *1 sc (UK dc) in next sp, 3 dc (UK tr) in next sp*, rep from * to * to end. Fasten off.

To make up
Work in the ends on all the pieces. Join the centre back seam of the top, slip it on to the bear, and join the shoulder seams. Sew a ribbon-and-rose bow to the front of the top. Sew a ribbon-and-rose bow to the centre front of each bootee and slip the bootees on to the bear's feet. Fold the diaper/nappy around the bear, tuck the end over the centre section and secure with a tiny safety pin.

Susie Sunshine Bear

Materials and equipment:

Crochet hook size 2.50mm (US B-1, UK 13)

No. 5 crochet cotton – 1 ball of dark brown

Small amounts of crochet cotton in beige, mid brown, white, yellow, gold and black

Black floss for embroidering features, and details on honey pot and bees

Toy stuffing

Sewing needle and threads in colours to match crochet cotton

Instructions:

Make the bear following the basic instructions at the beginning of the book, using dark brown for the head, body, arms and legs and beige for the muzzle and ears.

Honey pot

Row 1: using light brown, make 2 ch, 6 sc (UK dc) in 2nd ch from hook. Join in a circle with a sl st.

Row 2: 2 sc (UK dc) in each sc (UK dc) all round.

Row 3: *1 sc (UK dc) in next sc (UK dc), 2 sc (UK dc) in next sc (UK dc)*, rep from * to * all round.

Rows 4–6: working into back loops of sts only, 1 hdc (UK htr) in each sc (UK dc) all round, join with a sl st.

Row 7: *2 hdc (UK htr), hdc (UK htr) 2 tog*, rep from * to * to last 2 hdc (UK htr), 1 hdc (UK htr) in each of next 2 hdc (UK htr).

Rows 8 and 9: 1 sc (UK dc) in each hdc (UK htr) all round. Fasten off.

Honey-pot lid

Work rows 1–3 of pot, run thread up into centre of lid, make a large French knot on top of the lid to form the handle.

Honey

Using gold, work rows 1–3 of honey pot. Fasten off.

Label

Row 1: using beige, make 6 ch, 1 sc (UK dc) in 2nd ch from hook, 1 sc (UK dc) in each ch to end.

Rows 2–5: 1 sc (UK dc) in each sc (UK dc) to end, turn.

Fasten off.

Bees – body (make 2)

Row 1: using yellow, make 2 ch, 4 sc (UK dc) in 2nd ch from hook, join in a circle.

Rows 2–4: 1 sc (UK dc) in each sc (UK dc) all round, join.

Rows 5 and 6: join in black, work as rows 2–4, break yarn. Thread yarn through needle, draw up top of bee, sew through to make head.

Bees – wings (make 2)

Using white, make 6 ch, work 1 sl st in first ch, 5 ch, sl st in same place again. This forms two tiny loops. Fasten off, leaving long threads.

To make up

Work in the ends on all the honey-pot pieces. Stuff the honey pot lightly to give it a rounded shape. Slip the honey inside the top of the pot and sew it in place. Sew the label to the front of the honey pot and, using black floss, embroider the word 'honey' across the centre of the label. Stitch the honey-pot lid to the bear's paw, as shown opposite. Push the ends on each bee's body inside the body to lightly pad it. Stitch black lines around the body to form stripes using embroidery floss. Use the long threads on the wings to secure them to the bees' bodies. Work the ends through to the other side of the body and use them to secure one bee to the side of the honey pot and the other to the bear's shoulder.

Acknowledgements

Many thank go to Sirdar, Patons and DMC for kindly donating some of the yarns needed to create the bears. Thank you also to the team at Search Press for all their hard work in putting this book together and to the photographer for taking the wonderful photographs. Last but by no means least, a big thank you to my dear friends and family for all their encouragement, patience and inspiration.